Quilts With A View

A Fabric Adventure

by

Faye Labanaris

American Quilter's Society

P. O. Box 3290 • Paducah, KY 42002-3290

Located in Paducah, Kentucky, the American Quilter's Society (AQS) is dedicated to promoting the accomplishments of today's quilters. Through its publications and events, AQS strives to honor today's quiltmakers and their work and to inspire future creativity and innovation in quiltmaking.

EDITOR: BARBARA SMITH
BOOK DESIGN/ILLUSTRATIONS: LANETTE BALLARD
COVER DESIGN: MICHAEL BUCKINGHAM
PHOTOGRAPHY: CHARLES R. LYNCH

Library of Congress Cataloging-in-Publication Data

Labanaris, Faye.
   Quilts with a view: a fabric adventure / by Faye Labanaris.
                    p.   cm.
      ISBN 1-57432-713-5
      1. Appliqué.   2. Quilting.   3. Quilts--Design.   4. Textile fabrics
      in art.   I. Title.
TT779.L26   1998
746.44'5--dc21   98-43388
                                                   CIP

Additional copies of this book may be ordered from American Quilter's Society, PO Box 3290, Paducah, KY 42002-3290 @ $16.95. Add $2.00 for postage & handling.

Printed in the U.S.A. by Image Graphics, Paducah, KY

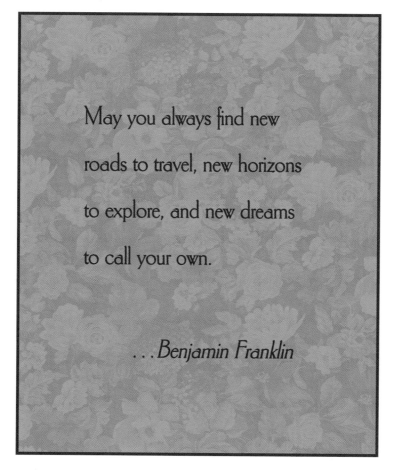

May you always find new

roads to travel, new horizons

to explore, and new dreams

to call your own.

...*Benjamin Franklin*

Dedicated to

Elizabeth Akana, who could not bear to cut

a beautiful piece of fabric and who started

me on this wonderful fabric adventure...

my students and lovers of fabric, for joining

me with excitement and creating wonderfully

original designs...

all the fabric designers for producing a never-

ending source of inspirational fabrics...

to all of you, a heartfelt thank you!

Acknowledgments

So many people, guilds, and quilt shops were a part of this fabric adventure that it would not be possible to list all of them here. I am very grateful for their support, encouragement, and excitement.

I would like to specifically thank the following people and organizations:

- Linda Hilliard, owner of Quilt Artisan, Middletown, Rhode Island, for first realizing the exciting potential of this concept.
- Dot Krueger, owner of Sew Crazy, Plymouth, Massachusetts, for offering me the loan of an Elna Sewing Machine and some basic machine lessons at just the right moment.
- Elna Sewing Machine Company for the loan of a sewing machine that opened my eyes to the wonder and ease of machine work.
- Husqvarna Viking Sewing Machine Company and Terry Smith for the loan of a Viking #1+ sewing machine for two years of almost effortless sewing and quilting.
- Mickey Lawler of Hartford, Connecticut, for her talent in creating such inspiring hand-painted fabrics: Skydyes.
- Ellen Peters of Laconia, New Hampshire, for being a very talented quilter, teacher, and friend. I could not have quilted so many quilts in such a short period of time as beautifully as she did.
- Marty Bowne of Mercer Island, Washington, for seeing the exciting potential in this concept and offering it as a joint class with Mickey Lawler at the 1997 pre-conference at Quilting by the Sound, Port Townsend, Washington, and to the great group of students who created so many wonderful quilts with their own hand-painted views.
- Eugenia Barnes of Marcellus, New York, for her historical expertise and appraisal skills.
- The American Quilter's Society and Meredith Schroeder for publishing this book with patience and understanding.
- Barbara Smith and Lauri Lynch Zadel, my editors, for their patience and editorial skills.
- Nick, Andrew, and Tom, husband and sons, for putting up with so much fabric and so little food during my bursts of creativity.
- And finally, to the fabric shops, for being there with the latest fabrics we just had to have.

Contents

Introduction

It all began quite innocently. What kind of gift does one quilter give another, especially when it is for a famous quilt teacher you've never met before? Fabric, of course. But the fabric had to be very special for such a person. So I chose to take hand-painted fabric to Elizabeth Akana in Hawaii. The year was 1991.

That was just the beginning of an exciting adventure that forever changed the way I looked at fabric. The adventure continued as I accompanied Elizabeth Akana during a 1994 teaching tour that took us to several New England states. During each class, she showed many samples of her work, some in the traditional Hawaiian quilting technique and some a bit more contemporary. She had one striking piece that especially caught my eye. Each time I saw it, I became more intrigued. It was a small wallhanging made from the piece of fabric I had given her. Elizabeth had not been able to cut into the hand-painted fabric because it was so beautiful, so she incorporated the whole piece into a simple but elegant design. I loved its unadorned beauty and its focus on the hand-painted fabric.

LOVE THROUGH THE WINDOW
25" x 32", by Elizabeth Akana, Kaneohe, Hawaii (1993); quilted by the author. This is the quilt that started it all.

I decided to make a similar piece. Just before we left for the last teaching engagement at the Quilt Artisan shop in Middletown, Rhode Island, we looked through my entire collection of Skydyes, hand-painted fabrics by Mickey Lawler of Connecticut. I arrived at the shop with a sewing basket full of beautiful, one-of-a-kind fabrics and a mind racing with renewed inspiration and excitement.

The Quilt Artisan is a wonderful shop bursting with gorgeous fabrics. I was excited about starting my newest project and began playing with bolts of fabric. The owner of the shop, my friend Linda Hilliard, had work to do, but her friend Mary Viti, who had stopped by to say hello, soon became interested in what I was doing. She helped me search for the perfect border. Finding the right fabric was no problem. We "threw" bolts of fabric on the carpeted floor to see how they looked bordering the hand-painted fabric. After we made our choices, we searched my fabric collection for more inspiration and spent the next few hours coming up with many more combinations.

I was really excited about these fabric-inspired designs. Many of my students had asked me what class I would teach next. Suddenly, I had the answer...a contemporary design class for people who thought they couldn't design but who really loved fabric. Linda offered me the opportunity to teach this new technique in a two-day class at her shop.

I started making samples for the class. Soon there were so many pieces ready to sew, I could not begin to hand appliqué and hand quilt them all, so I decided to use a sewing machine. After a few basic lessons, I actually enjoyed machine work. Twelve pieces were finished in two weeks. Doing it by hand, I would have completed only one or two quilts. The sewing machine, with its many stitches for quilting and appliqué, is the perfect partner for this fabric-inspired design technique.

My students always ask, "How do you know what fabric to use?" "Simply let it 'talk' to you," I tell them. We have all seen fabric we love. It starts speaking to you as soon as you see it, and your heart goes "Ahhhh!" This fabric adventure is a design process that takes its inspiration from the fabric. Basically, it is a fun and intuitive way to design. You don't really know what kind of quilt you are going to make until you have a piece of fabric in front of you. It's like eating popcorn – once you start, you can't stop. As one student (Kim Drake, Sunderland, Massachusetts) said after a class, "I loved it, I bought it, I couldn't cut it – but now I know what to do with it!"

In Chapter 1...

This chapter covers selecting fabrics for the three basic parts of your Quilt With A View.

Window frame
View fabric

It also covers the various types of window openings you can choose to make.

Chapter 1
Opening Windows

A WARNING TO FABRIC LOVERS: Proceed with caution! Neither the author nor the publisher will be responsible for the size of your fabric collection from this point on, and you will never look at fabric the same way again.

Getting Started Is Easy As 1-2-3!

1. Fabric

You will need at least three fabrics: one for a window frame, another for the view through the window, and a border fabric or two, or three, or more.

2. Basic Supplies

Clear template plastic

Rulers: 6" wide linear, and 12" square

Markers: chalk, chalk pencil, etc. (erasable)

Thread – matching and decorative

Milliner's (straw) or appliqué needles for hand appliqué

Small, sharp scissors that cut to the point

Pigma pen (.01) and freezer paper for inking

Fabric stabilizer or fusible material may be needed, depending on the appliqué method chosen

3. An Adventurous Spirit

Let the fabric talk to you.

Fabric Selection

I loved it! I bought it! I can't cut it! Now, what do I do with it?

Since fabrics are the starting point for this exciting technique, you may be concerned about choosing them. Don't worry. This is easy. Just choose the ones that speak to you – those fabrics that inspire you with their many intriguing possibilities. This can be exciting because there are so many new and wonderful fabrics coming on the market all the time. Why don't you put down this book for a few minutes and go to your collection (or the nearest fabric or quilt shop) to find a few of these special fabrics.

I'll bet that took you more than a few minutes. If your collection is anything like mine, you can't remember everything you've bought. Every time I look through my stash, I am re-introduced to my previous purchases. Some of them excite me, while others make me wonder why I bought them in the first place. We'll find a use for these fabrics, too, even if we have to use them for backing.

Basic Windows

STEP 1. CHOOSE A WINDOW FRAME: Let's begin with a small sample to show how the process works. Find a fat quarter or an 18" square with a medium- to small-scale floral print to use as a window frame. Don't worry about exact measurements. You can trim it later. Fold the fabric into quarters and press the creases to use as guidelines for centering the view fabric.

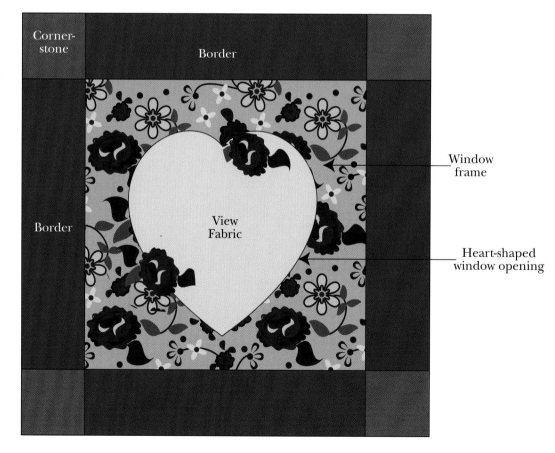

Basic parts of a Quilt With A View.

STEP 2. OPEN A WINDOW: Choose a basic shape, such as circle, oval, or heart. Cut the shape, approximately 9"–12" in diameter, from see-through template plastic. Place the template in the center of the fabric, using your pressed folds to find the center, and trace around the template with a chalk pencil or other marker. You can trace the template shape on the back of the fabric if you are afraid of marking the front, provided you can "read" the fabric design from the back. Cut out the shape, following the drawn line (Fig. 1). Remove the cut shape. You've just opened your first window.

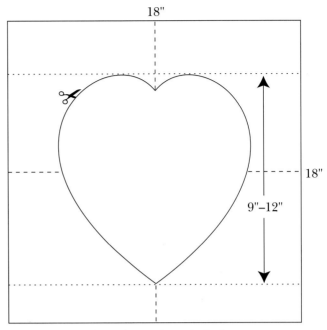

Figure 1. Opening a heart-shaped window.

STEP 3. AUDITION VIEW FABRICS: Select several fabrics to try out for the view through the window. But what are you looking for? You are looking for a special piece of fabric that will complement your window frame fabric, such as a beautiful hand-painted piece. Hand-painted fabrics are one-of-a-kind beauties that you just had to have, but because they are too pretty to cut, they just sit on your shelf. Now, you can use some of them. The fabric will not be cut into small pieces, but rather used whole-cloth so its full beauty can be seen and enjoyed. The view can also be a hand-dyed fabric, a wonderful Bali subtle print, or even a solid. It can even be a printed view right off the bolt.

You won't know if a view fabric will work until you place it under the window opening you've just cut. Look at the two fabrics together. No thinking and wondering allowed. Just stand back and look. You will have an instant reaction. If it's a ghastly combination, you will want to remove it quickly from your sight. If it's a "maybe," put it in a pile to study later. If it's just right, you will love it instantly. By trial and error, you'll eventually find the perfect view fabric. Don't rush this process, and don't worry. You'll find it.

Once you have found the right view for your window, pin the window and view fabrics together. If you don't pin them, you may lose the just-right view.

HELPFUL HINTS

Circle shapes can be drawn from household objects, such as a dinner plate or large pasta bowl. Oval shapes can easily be made by cutting a circle in half and connecting the halves with straight lines. Heart shapes can be made by cutting a half-heart shape from folded paper, bringing back fond memories of childhood valentines.

How much fabric do you leave around the window opening? If you are using a medium-scale print and an 18"–22" square of fabric, 3" should be enough from the cut edge of the motif to the center of the outside edge of the square (Fig. 2). Of course, more fabric can easily be left for larger quilts and less for small-scale miniatures.

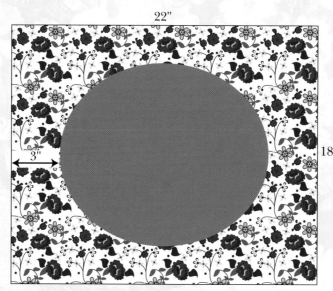

Figure 2. Leave at least 3" between the cut window and the outside edge of the window frame.

It's all a matter of scale. With a small-scale print, a fat quarter or less is enough. The smaller the fabric's scale, the less fabric you'll need for a window and the more regular in shape the window opening can be. A small-scale print lends itself to a simple opening, such as a circle, because the design is too small to obscure the line of the circle.

With a large-scale print, the reverse is true. The larger the scale of the print, the more apt you are to want to free-cut your window opening by simply following the fabric design motifs. You'll need at least one-half yard or more of fabric for a large print. (Turn to page 20 to learn about free-cut windows.)

More Windows

Once you have opened your first window with a basic shape, such as a circle, heart, or oval, you are ready to open a second window and explore the endless cutting possibilities based on the fabric's motifs. We'll proceed cautiously. After all, you are cutting into a piece of fabric you really love.

There are three cutting possibilities beyond using the basic shapes: broken-circle opening, free-cut opening, and wreath-cut opening.

BROKEN-CIRCLE OPENING

Use a medium- to large-scale print for this type of window, in which some of the fabric motifs are allowed to flow into the basic shape.

Trace a circular shape onto the front of your fabric with a chalk pencil or onto the back with a regular lead pencil. Because I prefer working on the front of the fabric, I am careful to use a chalk pencil that will erase completely once the line is no longer needed.

Look at the fabric's design to see which motifs break into the drawn circle. Determine which of the motifs you want to save and place a pin in each one to remind you to cut around it. Leaving a ¼" turn-under allowance by eye, cut around the saved motifs for part of the window, and follow the drawn circle between the motifs. The allowance can be trimmed off later if you decide to machine appliqué. In the meantime, the allowance will protect the cut edge from fraying until you are ready to sew. If you make a mistake and cut off too many motifs, don't worry. You can appliqué separate motifs wherever you want, to balance the design.

HELPFUL HINTS

How much of the basic shape should you leave when cutting the opening? When in doubt, work with the number three to balance your design. Leave three motifs. They do not have to be the same size.

Although the opening can be centered, you can also place the opening off-center for an asymmetrical design.

WILDFLOWERS

28" x 28", by the author; quilted by Ellen Peters.

This quilt is an example of a simple window opening. The circle template line is almost completely cut except for a bit of the window fabric's flowery foliage. A dark green-dyed view fabric echoes the leaf colors and provides a perfect background for embellishment. A wildflower bouquet from the fabric's print is brought into the view with embroidery and floral appliqué. You do not have to think about what to do, just look at the fabric's design and see what is there.

The floral border has a dark blue background, which balances the center dark fabric. The window frame and border were fighting each other until I added a narrow strip of rose and gold-flecked fabric. This strip neutralized the two prints and made them work together. To complete the piece, golden rays of sunshine were quilted in the view fabric. When in doubt about what to quilt, you can't go wrong with sunshine.

TEAHOUSE OF THE AUGUST MOON

25" x 25", by the author; view fabric hand-painted by Mickey Lawler.

This quilt illustrates the broken-circle opening very nicely. You can easily see the circle on the Oriental fabric and where the design breaks the line. A set of three bars in the lower-right section reminded me of a bridge, so that was left in place. A cloud in the upper-left section was also kept, along with a softer set of bars to balance the opening.

I chose a beautiful, hand-painted, soft sunrise sky for the view fabric. The colors in the window frame fabric are echoed in the view fabric and in the border. A 1" wide strip of raw silk, hand-dyed by Susan Kinkki of Kauai, Hawaii, provided the perfect accent strip to unite the border and view fabric.

The inspiration for embellishing this piece to unite the border and view fabric came from the small floral sprays and branches in the window fabric. These design elements were echoed in the view area with buttons, beads, and embroidery. When it was time to quilt the view area, I made a template of a cloud with a few of the bars, which became the quilting motif for the sky. I hand quilted the view fabric with a gold metallic thread to represent sunshine.

Broken-Circle Opening

FERN GLEN

24" x 24", by the author; view fabric hand-painted by Mickey Lawler.

A heart template was used as the cutting guide. A few of the fabric's design motifs were left uncut to break into the heart shape. The view fabric was a sun print of actual ferns. This piece of fabric provides just the right view, so no further embellishment is necessary.

A decorative machine embroidery stitch outlines the heart-shaped opening, adding a subtle bit of interest. The border size was determined by a small piece of hand-dyed purple fabric, cut into four equal lengths. Four squares of view fabric were added as cornerstones to complete the border. The simplicity of the piece enhances the fabrics used.

Plum Blossom

28" x 28", by the author.

Here is another example of the broken-circle technique. A fabric with an Oriental design was the basis for this piece. You can see the basic circle line and where the fabric motifs broke the line to become part of the opening. A solid-green, polished chintz was used as the view fabric.

Branches embroidered with a rose-colored silk buttonhole-twist thread contrast nicely with the dark green background. Bead and button embellishments complete the branches. The view fabric is hand quilted with gold metallic thread, following the meandering stream design in the Oriental fabric. Machine quilting continues on the window fabric's main design lines. More beading on the flowers in the window fabric unites the design and the embellishments. I selected a decorator chintz in colors similar to those in the window fabric for the border. A narrow strip of a calico floral provides an accent color for the border.

QUEEN LILI'UOKALANI'S GARDEN, HILO, HAWAII

54" x 36", by the author.

FREE-CUTTING METHOD

No template is used for this technique. Simply cut your window opening following the fabric motifs. This method works best with half- to full-yard pieces that have medium- to large-scale prints. Leave at least 6" of material around the window opening. To cut the opening, just meander with your scissors. The opening does not have to be symmetrical. Motifs may be cut from the center of the fabric and placed wherever needed to enhance the window frame.

This quilt is an example of getting carried away with cutting. I was having so much fun following the intricate designs that, before I realized it, I had cut open a full yard. The view is made from a half-yard hand-painted piece. The raw edge of the window frame is machine appliquéd with a variegated metallic thread to echo the metallic design in the fabric. A floral stripe with the same colors as the window fabric proved to be just right for a border.

MEMORIES OF ALOHA

64" round, by the author.

WREATH-CUTTING METHOD

For this method, start by cutting a floral fabric, following the flower motifs to form a circular center opening. Next, cut a larger circle around the first one, using the fabric's motifs as your guide to create a wreath. This is the ultimate scissors exercise in free-cutting. It's fun to use this cutting method on large-scale floral prints.

This is an example of a quilt that kept talking to me during its construction. It began as a 16" block for a Baltimore album class. I used Elizabeth Akana's ISLAND GIRL pattern and added a ruched lei. The piece looked lonely, so I decided to add a floral border cut along the flower motifs to soften the center block. That was so much fun that, before I knew it, the ISLAND GIRL was surrounded with a lei of tropical flowers.

The next border was again softened by cutting along the motifs. So I added ruched leis where the design touched the sun fabric. How to bind the piece became a stumbling block. It didn't feel right to cut a straight line through the motifs, so I turned the batting and backing under along the motifs' outer edges. When this step was completed, the quilt still did not feel finished, so I added a couched gold braid to the outer edge to represent sunshine.

WORKING BACKWARD

Wonderful fabrics simulating sunrises, sunsets, and skies in various moods and dramatic colors lend themselves beautifully and quite naturally as view fabrics. These fabrics are one-of-a-kind works of art and are too precious to cut into small pieces. By using them whole-cloth, they appear almost in their entirety. This type of fabric makes your quilt come to life.

This leads us to another technique for opening a window – working backward. Previously, you started with an inspiring window fabric, then found an appropriate view fabric. Now, you will begin with a beautiful view fabric and search through your collection for an appropriate window frame fabric. The fabrics need not be the same size or shape.

Once you have chosen your fabrics, they can be folded and pressed in quarters to aid in centering them (Fig. 3). Center the view fabric, right side down, on the wrong side of the window frame fabric. The wrong sides of both fabrics will be facing you. Pin the view fabric in place (Fig. 4). With a contrasting thread, baste ½" in from the outside edge all around the view fabric (Fig. 5). The basted line will show the dimensions of the view fabric underneath the window. Turn the fabrics over to the right side (Fig. 6). Place a pin in the window motifs you want to save (Fig. 7). Carefully cut away the window frame fabric, exposing as much of the view fabric as you like (Fig. 8).

This is not as hard as it sounds. To start, cut carefully and conservatively. You can always cut away more later. Keep the view fabric pulled away from the cutting area and the scissors pointed upward to avoid cutting the view fabric. Duckbilled appliqué scissors can be used successfully here.

You can also cut beyond the basted area where there is no view fabric. Use scraps of view fabric from your stash to extend the view beyond the basting stitches.

If you do cut away too much window fabric, you can simply appliqué additional motifs over those areas.

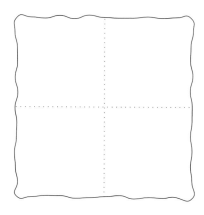

Figure 3. Fold window frame and view fabrics to find their centers.

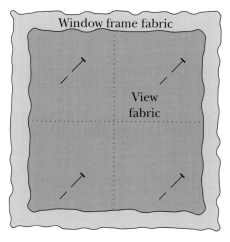

Figure 4. Lay view fabric on top of window frame fabric, both wrong sides facing you.

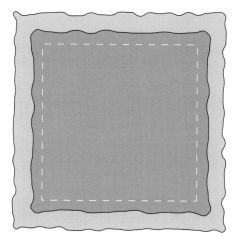

Figure 5. Baste ½" in from the outside edge of the view fabric on the wrong side.

Figure 6. Turn fabrics right side up. Basting stitches show outline of view fabric.

Figure 7. Use pins to mark the motifs you want to save.

Figure 8. Cut away the window frame to expose the view.

RIVER IN THE SKY

33" x 24", by the author; quilted by Ellen Peters; view fabric hand-painted by Mickey Lawler.

This delightful little quilt began with a piece of orange hand-painted fabric with a streak of sparkly blue. Because I wanted to use all of the fabric as the view, I developed the working-backward technique.

I selected a floral fabric with tropical orange flowers for the window. Once the basting and cutting were completed, I was pleased to see that almost all of the view fabric had been exposed. I added a simple picture-frame border with a purple accent strip and an inked detail of a hula dancer on a cliff.

MY GARDEN VIEW OF PARADISE

36" x 37", by Anita Askins, Annapolis, Maryland.

LAYERED LANDSCAPES

These landscape views are constructed by appliquéing layers of fabrics. Dozens of wonderful fabrics are available to use as mountains, water, etc., or you can use some simple, basic shapes cut from fabric. The effect you want is achieved by the fabrics you select.

Layered landscapes are a bit more complex and require some thought, but they are well worth your time. The window fabric provides the framework that surrounds the landscape view.

"While on vacation one year, my husband and I were driving outside Honolulu and stopped to climb down a bank to a cove," Anita says. "This quilt is my depiction of Diamond Head as I saw it from that cove."

Anita's layered landscape quilt shows the use of basic shapes and the effective use of fabric to represent the landscape components of mountains, sea, shore, water, palm tree, and the glint of sun on a sail. A sunny yellow accent strip separates a border that represents the colors of lava.

Layered Cut-Out Shapes
THE TRINITY ALPS

28" x 29", by Patricia Nelson, Athens, Pennsylvania.

Patricia created a beautiful layered landscape view inside her window of autumn foliage. The landscape has layered mountain ranges in five different shades of blue, giving the viewer the illusion of distance. Machine-embroidered details, such as the trees at the shoreline and cattails in the foreground, as well as the embellished flowers and foliage made with thread lace, create a delightful view that invites one to linger.

My "Bali Hai"

46" x 34", by Patricia A. Murray, Honolulu, Hawaii.

A beautiful large fabric of a hand-painted ocean and sunset was Patricia's inspiration for this island view. She chose a floral bark cloth for the outer border. The center was carefully cut out, and in its place is a hand-painted sky-ocean fabric. Patricia machine appliquéd mountains on the horizon and inked in trees and other mountains. She then hand appliquéd additional leaves and flowers and machine quilted the rest of the quilt in gold metallic thread.

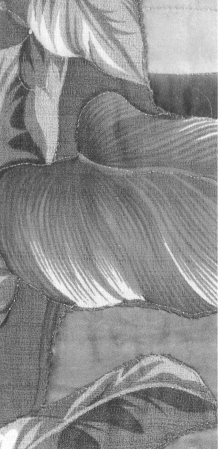

"I loved the freedom to create and individualize a vision by innovative use of fabric," Patricia explains. "I loved the idea of inviting the viewer to come closer and be a part of something special that I created. As a Hawaiian, I enjoy being surrounded by lush flowers, mountains, and oceans, but the opportunity to let the fabric take me away was a pleasure indeed."

Miniature with Oval Opening

CHICKADEE-DEE-DEE

13" x 18", by Doris Gage-West, Brewster, Massachusetts.

MINIATURES

Small-scale prints lend themselves to miniature windows and landscapes. These pocket-size pieces, delightfully small, are quick and easy to make.

There is no end to the design potential inspired by fabrics. You are limited only by the fabrics you have on hand or will have after your next shopping trip.

For Doris, the scale of the chickadee print dictated that the finished quilt be a miniature. Because curves are softer than straight lines, Doris decided to use an oval window. Once the quilt had been put together, it was apparent to her that something was missing, leading her to add another chickadee looking out the window at his buddies. The branches lent themselves naturally to embroidered extensions into the dark red border, where tiny beads repeat the berries. "This concept challenged me to think about fabrics from a different point of view - to take the fabric and work out a design, rather than my usual style of working out the design, then looking for the fabric," Doris says.

Marylou created this quilt after she had to miss the class I presented to her sewing group. Class notes and samples shown to her a few days later inspired her to give it a try. She has long enjoyed stitching miniatures in cross-stitch, so it was no surprise that she would create a miniature window. She selected a printed grapevine wreath fabric and added a singing bird in its center. A leftover piece of hand-painted fabric makes the perfect sky for the center. Silk-ribbon embroidered roses and French knots complete the view.

Australian Sunrise

26" x 26", by Marguerite Danowski, Silver Spring, Maryland.

"My quilt, made with very small pieces of fabrics printed in Australia, is a pleasant reminder of my trip there. The fabrics depict animals and scenery in Australia," Marguerite says.

We all love to shop for fabrics, especially when we're on vacation. It's fun to explore quilt shops in all parts of the world and bring home some fabric for special remembrance projects, such as Australian Sunrise.

WHOLE-CLOTH LANDSCAPES

What view from a window is more natural than a landscape. There are several methods for constructing these landscape views, from quick whole-cloth cutting to fabric layering. Look carefully in your fabric collection. The right fabrics may be just waiting for you.

Whole-cloth landscape scenes printed on fabric provide a quick and easy view (see IN THE BEGINNING on the next page). Shopping for this fabric is the only effort involved. Perhaps you have been ignoring these prints because you didn't know what to do with them. Well, now is your chance to use them.

Look at a landscape print and decide just how much of the scene you want to use. A clear template or square ruler can help you visualize the size of scene you want. Cut the landscape to the desired size, then surround it with an appropriate border. The quilt is complete in just a few easy steps.

FIREWORKS OVER PROVENCE, see page 34.

Whole-Cloth Landscape
In the Beginning
31" x 22", by Corrine Linscott, Lyman Maine.

In this quilt, Corrine placed the lagoon fabric on top of an electric sky border of similar colors. A portion of the lagoon, cut along the mountain outline with waves on the edges, was appliquéd in the center of the printed stormy sky. A narrow accent of green was inserted to separate the view fabric from the sky, creating a simple yet dynamic presentation.

MORNING IN MAUI

36" x 44", by the author; quilted by Ellen Peters.

LINEAR LANDSCAPES

This landscape view consists of only two or three basic components and is constructed in a stacked or linear manner. It begins with a whole-cloth landscape scene printed on fabric. The scene is the starting point for the view. It is cut into a wide strip with the exact width determined by the scene. Pieces of fabric are added for the sky, land, and water, and…1-2-3…it's done. You may want to add a border or leave it as is. Whatever you decide, the result is a wonderful landscape quilt you have created very quickly.

MORNING IN MAUI is a three-part landscape quilt. A great piece of Hawaiian shirt fabric, a sky fabric, and a whale print complete the view. Naming the quilts is almost as much fun as creating them. Although I have never been to Maui to see the whales when they migrate from Alaska to give birth. I can imagine that a morning in Maui would be like this.

Linear Landscape
Fireworks Over Provence
44" x 42", by the author; quilted by Ellen Peters.

A dramatic African sateen fabric of sunbursts was the inspiration for this quilt. A base fabric of village houses and vineyards and the vine canopy of grapes complete the piece. I originally titled it "Morning, Noon, and Night" to represent tending the vineyards in France. However, most people commented on the fireworks in the sky, hence the title change. The sunbursts provided an excellent opportunity for elaborate beading of the fireworks displays.

STRIPPIE TOPS

Over 100 years ago, printed fabrics, paisleys, and chintzes were expensive. To stretch the fabrics, they were cut into long strips and stitched with plain cotton fabric strips in between. These strippie quilts were easy to do, and they allowed the beauty of the chintzes to be seen.

Today's fabrics, with compatible colors and themes, can be combined in strips reminiscent of the old strippie quilts. This technique results in a large quilt top in a short time with little effort. The potential for quilting stitches and background fabrics give the maker many opportunities to be creative (see OCEAN BLUE on the next page).

1 + 3 = 4-PATCH

Another basic patchwork design that was common with early quilters was the four-patch block. To apply the fabric-inspired design process to the four-patch idea, you can start with a theme, you can use a block you have already made, or you can start with an inspirational piece of fabric. Add three additional fabrics to complete the four-patch design (see MADAME PELE on page 37).

HELPFUL HINTS

Why limit yourself when there's a whole exciting world of textiles to choose from. Brocade ribbons, tapestries, and ethnic fabrics are just a few of the exotic materials available for inspiring original creations.

The use of antique fabrics and other textiles opens another window of opportunity. The selection of an antique textile as a starting point for a block design or an accent gives a new lease on life to forgotten pieces tucked away on your shelves. For instance, consider using embroidered textiles as focal points, borders, or backgrounds in your Quilts With A View.

OCEAN BLUE

54" x 78", by the author; quilted by Ellen Peters.

A one-yard piece of shaded water fabric inspired this quilt. Since the one-yard piece was all I had and I didn't want to waste any of it, I cut it into three equal pieces from selvage to selvage to get the complete fabric design in each piece.

On my fabric shelf, I found a batiked fish print in similar colors. That piece was also cut into equal strips. The result was a strippie top. I then added several border strips of shell fabric to the bottom to widen the quilt and to make it visually more interesting by breaking up the strong vertical lines. The backing fabric, a large-scale, multi-colored, tropical fish print, relates to the theme of the top. Quilting lines of water and fish from the backing fabric unify the various fabrics into a single piece. The result was a quick to make, large-scale quilt.

MADAME PELE

48" x 38", by the author; quilted by Ellen Peters; beaded by Kate Carroll; view fabric hand-painted by Mickey Lawler.

This quilt started with an appliquéd block made for a guild challenge on the elements earth, air, fire, and water. The block represents fire. The figure is Madame Pele, the goddess of the volcano. The drawing of her, inked by my son Andrew, was based on a postcard by Hawaiian artist Herb Kane.

The block was an orphan for about a year before I decided to expand it. I had purchased a magnificent hand-painted piece of fabric that reminded me of lava flowing into the ocean. I positioned this fabric below the Pele block, and the result was exciting. Two additional fabrics were soon found to complete my four-patch. These fabrics represent a sunset sky and underwater sea life. They were joined by appliquéing a meandering line to create a unified appearance. Only the horizon line where the sky meets the ocean was sewn as a straight line.

The quilt has no border or straight outer lines. The lower right corner was cut to represent two tongues of lava flowing into the ocean. This cut was made by Nina Mederios of Kauai, Hawaii. When she saw the top before it was quilted, she told me the lava flow should have two pathways, so I handed her a pair of scissors and let her cut it. The quilt was quilted with metallic threads.

In Chapter 2 ...

This chapter covers the various ways you can assemble your Quilt With A View.

Chapter 2

Simple Assembly

Once you have decided on the type of Quilt With A View you want and have chosen your fabrics, the pieces are ready to be sewn together. There are several ways to accomplish this. You may want to experiment with a combination of methods.

Window Appliqué

NO-SEW WINDOWS

This cut-and-paste method is the easiest of all because no sewing skills are needed. There are quite a few fusible products on the market, and your quilt shop will be able to assist you in selecting one to meet your needs. First, gather a sharp pair of scissors, an iron, and some fusible backing. Next, place the fusible material on the back of the window fabric and fuse according to the manufacturer's directions. Cut out the window. Peel off the paper from the fusible material and fuse the window fabric onto the view fabric to complete the quilt. This method is an excellent choice for beginners who haven't mastered traditional forms of appliqué; for making quick quilts to give as gifts; or for children, under the supervision of an adult, who want to make a first quilt.

NEEDLE-TURN APPLIQUÉ

The beauty of hand appliqué is that it makes a project completely portable so it can be stitched anywhere. However, if the window opening is fairly large, you may want to use machine appliqué to save time.

The right sewing needle makes all the difference. There are several kinds that can be used. Quilting needles (betweens) are about 1" long and require a bit of dexterity to use for appliqué. I quilt with a #12 and have no trouble at all with this needle when quilting, but I am all thumbs when I use this needle for appliqué. Appliqué needles (sharps) are about 1¼" long. Their length gives a bit more control for needle-turning. However, I prefer to use a milliners or straw needle for my hand appliqué work. These needles are 1½" long, quite thin, and make needle-turning a breeze. They may be a bit unwieldy at first, but give them a chance.

Use a single strand of fine thread (about 18" long and knotted) that matches the color of the appliqué rather than the background. If the fabric has many colors, use a neutral gray thread.

Small, sharp scissors, such as embroidery scissors, are just right for cutting away fabric close to a design area. Large scissors do not give you the tip-cutting control you need for hard-to-cut areas.

Prepare the window fabric by cutting the window shape, leaving ¼", by eye, for a turn-under allowance. Always leave a little more allowance than is actually needed. It can be trimmed once you start sewing.

Trim the turn-under allowance to about ⅛" as you sew. If you cut too far ahead of your needle, you will have difficulty turning the edge under. You will continually be fighting the fabric to make it stay in place. The just-right amount to cut will soon be evident after a few stitches. (Please note: If you are right-handed, you will stitch to your left. The reverse is true for left-handed quilters.)

For the appliqué stitch, bring the knotted thread from the back of the window fabric to the front, coming up at the edge of the window. Use the tip of the needle to push the fabric under along the edge. Take a few tiny stitches to anchor the window to the background fabric. With needle-turning, the tip of the needle is used to grab the turn-under allowance about 1" from the anchoring stitches (Fig. 9). Push the allowance under with the tip of the needle and slide the allowance under with the side of the needle (Fig. 10). Hold the turned-under fabric in place with your left thumb. Take one stitch at a time, stitching to about half of the turned-under distance. Turn under another 1" of raw edge, hold, and stitch half the distance again. This will result in smooth edges. If you stitch right up to your thumb, you will end up with pointy curves.

To make an appliqué stitch, come up in the fold of the appliqué fabric, then straight down into the background fabric. For the second stitch, the needle is brought up into the fold of the appliqué fabric and a little to the left of the previous stitch. Continue to stitch, adding about three stitches every ¼" around the window. With a little practice, you'll be comfortable with the rhythm and ease of this method.

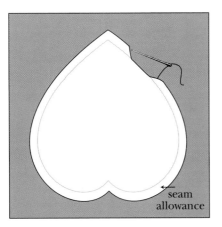

Figure 9. Use needle tip to grab and turn under the allowance.

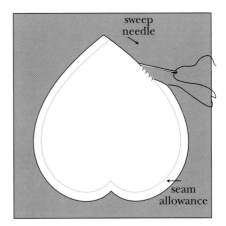

Figure 10. Slide the allowance under with tip of needle.

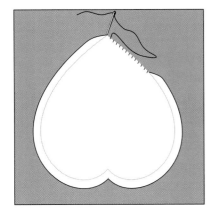

Figure 11a. First fold for points.

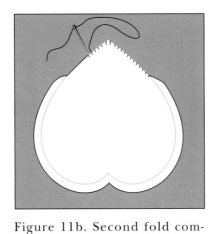

Figure 11b. Second fold completes the point.

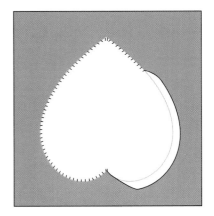

Figure 12. Take two stitches in the V.

PEAKS AND VALLEYS. Inside and outside corners are not hard to master with needle-turn appliqué. With a point, you'll needle-turn almost to the tip, stopping about ⅛" away from the tip. Take a couple of appliqué stitches in place at the tip. You have just stitched half of the point. Use the tip of the needle, a wooden toothpick, or the points of your small scissors to push or fold the remaining fabric under at an angle, almost like you are wrapping a Christmas present or making a hospital fold in a bed sheet (Fig. 11a & b). Give the thread a little tug, and the fabric will be pulled into a point. Take a few more tiny stitches on this side of the point, turn under the next length of fabric and continue sewing. You will stitch a perfect point every time.

For inside corners, as you approach the *V* center, make your stitches closer together to hold the fabric in place. Take a couple of stitches in the center of the *V* to hold the raw edge and to keep the *V*-shape (Fig. 12).

MACHINE APPLIQUÉ *by Ellen Peters*

Machine appliqué can be done with raw or turned edges. For raw-edge appliqué, cut out the pieces, leaving no turn-under allowance. Turned-edge appliqué includes an allowance that is turned under and secured with invisible or decorative stitching.

RAW-EDGE APPLIQUÉ. Fraying of raw edges can be avoided in several ways:
1. Apply a fusible web to the wrong side of the fabric before cutting the pieces. Some do not like to use fusible web because it makes the fabric stiff and hard to quilt. Fusing a narrow strip around only the edge of the fabric keeps the piece more pliable.
2. Use a liquid fusible on the raw edges after cutting.
3. Machine sew the pieces to the background with a tight buttonhole or satin stitch.

TURNED-EDGE APPLIQUÉ. Use your favorite method to turn the allowance under and secure it with a basting stitch. Hand basting is easier than machine basting. Secure the appliqué piece to the background with a machine stitch.

You can choose several machine stitches. The invisible stitch is created by using the blind-hem stitch with "invisible" nylon thread in the needle and regular thread in the bobbin. You may need to loosen the tension for the nylon. You can also use a zigzag stitch or one of the decorative stitches on your machine. Before using a decorative stitch, try a sample appliqué to learn how to handle the machine on twists and turns in the design. Another method of securing the appliqués to the background is to drop the feed dogs, use a darning foot, and guide the piece through free-hand.

CURVES AND POINTS. If a curve is tight, it may be necessary to stop sewing with the needle down, lift the presser foot and move the fabric over a bit, to continue sewing, sometimes as often as every stitch on very tight curves. For points, test decorative stitches on scrap fabric. The simpler stitches, such as zigzag and satin stitch, will be easier to control at a point.

Borders...Basic and Beyond

To border or not to border...that is the question. Once the window and view fabrics have been appliquéd together, you need to decide on a border. You can dig into your fabric collection for the appropriate fabrics to use. There are several border options to consider.

NO BORDERS

Some pieces require only binding to finish. The window and view require no other framework. MORNING IN MAUI, page 33, is a linear landscape that needs no borders.

ONE-FABRIC BORDERS

Border fabrics that will enhance your quilt can easily be determined by trial and error, a quilter's standard method of operation. Fold a piece of complementary fabric lengthwise to approximate width of border (a 6" width is a good place to start) and place it next to your window piece to audition it. Don't think about what might go together. Simply select fabrics of a similar or complementary color. If you start to think about matching your selections, you will only slow the process down. Just select, place, and look. If it looks right, then it is right. If you are hesitant about whether your selected border fabric works, stand back and view it from a distance. You will have the same reactions as when you were making view fabric decisions: ghastly, maybe, or just right.

ACCENT STRIPS

A narrow strip of fabric, sewn between the window and border fabric, can serve as an accent. It can be as narrow as a ⅛" piping or as wide as a ½" strip. If it is any wider, it will no longer function as an accent strip but will look like another border. The accent strip acts as a neutralizer, tying the border and window fabrics together. Since it is so narrow, it can be a really powerful fabric. It is amazing how such a small strip can make two fabrics work together. Before you disregard any fabric for your borders, add a narrow accent piece. You may be pleasantly surprised.

A second strip of the same fabric can be added as an accent outside the border. Sometimes the binding fabric acts as an accent strip and completes the framing. Striped fabrics can make great borders and accent strips. They add just enough spice to your basic fabric selections. QUEEN LILI'UOKALANI'S GARDEN, HILO, HAWAII, page 20, utilizes a striped fabric for the border.

ELABORATE BORDERS

When a basic border is just too simple, an elaborate border is the answer. The desired effect can be achieved through fabric selection. For example, you can choose hand-painted cotton, tapestry, velvet, or metallic fabrics. Borders can also be elaborate in their construction: pieced, appliquéd, or crazy quilted with antique fabrics, laces, and trims.

If you've exhausted yourself in searching for just the right fabric in your collection, then you'll have to rest up a bit before going to the store for that perfect border fabric you know is just waiting for you. Soon, you'll be back with many new pieces, because who can leave a shop with only one.

FORGET-ME-NOT

21" x 21", by the author.

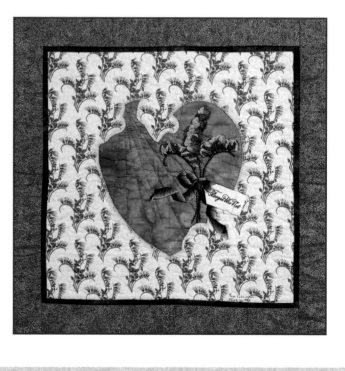

FORGET-ME-NOT has a double strip of dark green that accents the pink picture-frame border. The dark green also binds the piece. This quilt has a simple heart-shaped window opening, and it is edged with a decorative machine buttonhole stitch. The dyed green fabric makes a perfect background for a bouquet of dimensional French ribbon flowers inspired by the flowers in the fabric's design. A blue ribbon bow ties the bouquet together, and a calligraphic note of remembrance is appliquéd onto the bouquet.

JUST BELOW THE SURFACE

42" x 32", by Melanie Crane, Biddeford, Maine; fabric hand-painted by Mickey Lawler.

APPLIQUÉD WHOLE-CLOTH BORDER

If the fabric you have chosen for a border is too beautiful to cut into strips, you can cut a window in it and appliqué it in place, creating a window within a window. These borders are best made from a large-scale floral or foliage fabric. The working-backward technique, described on page 22, would apply to the construction of this border.

Melanie's quilt is an excellent example of the effective use of several border fabrics. She used almost a full yard of a large-scale print of tropical fish for the window fabric, in which she cut a large irregular opening for an ocean view. A stunning hand-painted cotton fabric with wonderful streaks of orange against a blue background was cut in half and placed on either side of the fish fabric to convey the feeling of fish swimming. The window opening was cut to include a few fish swimming into the border edges.

A top border of sky was added to show the tranquillity below the waves while a storm brews above. The fish swim placidly through the seaweed as lightning flashes in the clouds. The bottom border is a combination of a seaweed fabric with additional pieces of seaweed fused in place and with several more fish added to continue the effect.

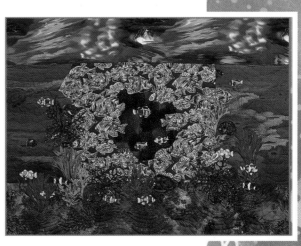

DOWN THE GARDEN PATH

29" x 20", by the author.

A variety of borders adds interest to this quilt. It was inspired by a packet of challenge fabric issued to the members of my guild. As soon as I saw the one with the garden chairs, I opened a window in it and placed a view of blue sky behind it. The rest of the fabrics in the packet became a series of borders representing parts of the garden: the latticed trellis work with blooms behind it, a brick pathway with dimensional prairie-point bricks as an edging, a border of assorted flower beds, a section of lawn, and a dark shrub border.

An inked trellis with silk-ribbon-embroidered blooms highlights the view into the garden. An inked birdbath and birds complete the detail work, taking the viewer into the garden and beyond.

LITTLE BIRD IN THE WINDOW

36" x 36", by Jane E. Hamilton, Kennett Square, Pennsylvania;
view fabric hand-painted by Mickey Lawler.

This quilt is a wonderful example of going beyond basic borders. It conveys a love of nature, a love of fabric, and a love of design.

It was completed in February 1997 for the American Quilter's Society Nursery Rhyme Challenge. The label contains the nursery rhyme "Once I Saw a Little Bird." The piece depicts a bird silhouetted against the sunset, as birds are often seen. Jane explains, "Originally, I was going to incorporate a dozen bright orange, red, and purple friendship blocks into the piece. However, while perusing my fabric stash one day, I ran across a beautiful fabric I knew would work for a sunset.

"The upper-right section of the window was not closed by fabric but left open to show the freedom of flight birds have and the tranquillity of the heavens. The piece dictated its own border. I designed and pieced an intricate border with a multitude of fabrics. Many parts of the quilt are quilted with metallic threads."

WILSON'S POND REMEMBERED

35" x 43", by Trish Robbins, West Chester, Pennsylvania.

"Wilson's pond was down the dirt road from my grandparents' farm," Trish says. "As children, we romped in the fields, fed the pigs, and played with the tadpoles at the pond. This scene reminds me of happy childhood experiences that I will never forget."

Trish's center window block with its irregular opening and landscape view of a pond against a hand-painted sunset sky was the basis for a round-robin with her quilting bee, the Material Girls. There is a great deal of embellishment with beading and buttons and decorative stitching on the many-themed blocks scattered throughout the border, as well as a lot of memories, fabric, and fun.

OH, TO BE IN ENGLAND

32" x 44", by the author.

This quilt has an attic-window-style border framing the view. A wood-printed fabric used for the bottom and one side, and a flower border appliquéd on the top and a side, give the illusion of viewing the English countryside through the window of a vine-covered cottage. The flowers in the large-scale floral print have been cut to overlap the window view.

In Chapter 3...

This chapter covers various methods for appliquéing, enhancing, and finishing your Quilt With A View.

Embellishments, 51
Pen and ink, 54
Finishing, 58

Embellishing and Finishing

After your borders are stitched, you are ready to enhance the piece with embellishments. These details are like dessert after a meal – a lot or a little, it's all up to you. The fabric's design will be your guide for the embellishment of the piece.

Embellishments

You can isolate a single motif from the window fabric to use as an accent. The motif can be recreated with French wire-edged ribbon blooms, embroidery, or fabric to emphasize the fabric's design element. (See FORGET-ME-NOT on page 44 for an example of simple embellishments.)

The accent can be taken directly from the fabric's design and translated into silk-ribbon embroidery or fine appliqué. Use beads and buttons to enhance this gentle accent treatment.

Elaborate accents of either appliquéd fabric or dimensional flowers can make a bold statement. The flowers created can be inspired by the flowers in your fabric's design. Again, the fabric will tell you what to do.

The use of a permanent fabric pen can add greater detail to a view than can be achieved with embroidery. Some quilts lend themselves to verses of poetry or quotations. These can be added separately on an inked banner or scroll, which is then appliquéd to the quilt top in an appropriate spot.

THE GIFT OF A LETTER

22" x 22", by the author; quilted by Ellen Peters.

A large bouquet of flowers made from French wire-edged ribbon and fabric creates a central accent to this fabric-inspired design. A bow of real ribbon ties the bouquet and message to the piece. A simple picture-frame border completes this valentine view.

THESE ARE A FEW OF MY FAVORITE THINGS: HOFFMANS, BLOOMS, AND HUMMINGBIRD WINGS

26" x 26", by Debbie Eaton, Groton, Massachusetts.

"I've always wanted to capture the view of the hummingbirds outside of my window," Debbie says. "I'm now looking to my fabric to inspire me instead of coming up with an idea and trying to find the right fabric later. I'm even noticing a whole new world through the windows in my house."

Debbie embellished a pure circle window opening, against a plain ivory background, with an elaborate appliquéd arching vine of flowers and several hummingbirds in flight. She effectively used shaded fabric and beaded accents for the blooms and a striped fabric for the hummingbirds' wings and bodies.

Pen and Ink

Writing on fabric is not to be feared! Wonderful results can be yours if you take a few minutes to practice on a scrap of fabric before using a fabric pen on your project. Here are a few basic tips that will help you to use ink beautifully and fearlessly.

Always pre-test all marking pencils and pens on the fabrics you are planning to use. Marking tools vary in their chemical makeup, and fabrics vary as to chemical dye and finish, so there is no way to predict how a marker and a fabric will react together. Begin with a .01 pen, and soon you'll want to try various marking widths and colors.

To test a marker, touch the pen to a corner of the fabric. If the spot remains as a dot, you can easily work with the ink on that fabric. However, if the spot spreads, then you'll have to make a decision. Either change the fabric or practice writing with a very light touch to keep the ink from being absorbed by the fabric. I do not pre-wash fabrics because that would soften the texture and remove the glazed surface, which I prefer for inking.

Practice drawing or writing on a piece of paper first to determine proper spacing and general appearance. You can make preliminary drawings or letters on fabric with a hard mechanical lead pencil (.05). Write with a very light touch. First test the pencil to be sure it erases from your fabric. Also test the eraser to see that it leaves no marks. An eraser smudge will not come out easily. With a light touch, gently ink over the pencil lines. You may have to go over them several times. Allow to air dry, then heat-set with an iron.

You can press freezer paper, shiny side down, on the back of your fabric after you have completed the preliminary drawing. Use a hot iron on a hard surface, such as a fabric-covered board. The freezer paper will stabilize the fabric, which makes inking easier.

Shade the letters in the words by thickening the down stroke for a calligraphic look (Fig. 13). Without this step, your penmanship will look like inked chicken scratches, no matter how beautiful your writing is. Again, practice this technique on scrap fabric until you are comfortable with the process.

Figure 13. Thicken the down stroke for more beautiful writing.

WITCH WAY TO WHITMAN

25" x 24", by Deborah Carye; view fabric by Mickey Lawler.

This whimsical piece with a holiday flavor provided Deborah with a great way to use novelty fabrics. She carried the theme of the fabric's design to the window opening by cutting a pumpkin shape and letting some of the pumpkins break the cutting line. An exciting hot orange and yellow sunset sky fabric was a perfect choice for the view. Deborah completed the theme by stenciling the outline of a witch on a broom in the sky, then inking it in for a black silhouette against the sunset.

Tree Drawing in Ink

CHISHOLM TRAIL

25" x 25", by Georgette Sutton, Biddeford, Maine.

Georgette started CHISHOLM TRAIL with a circle opening on a piece of plain green fabric. Her view is a light gray mountain range, which she found on a printed fabric right off the bolt.

She emphasized the feeling of the forest by inking in a large tree. The branches flow into the mountain view, tying the entire scene together. An accent strip of night-sky blue fabric separates the border of spring wildflowers.

CASTLE VISTA

26" x 26", by Fern Junnila, Centerville, Massachusetts.

Details in the view do not have to be inked or elaborately appliquéd. CASTLE VISTA is an excellent example of the effectiveness of a simple triangle shape. This shape representing a sail on the horizon carries the viewer through the floral arbor, over the stone arch, across the sand dunes, and out to sea. You can almost feel the wind in the sails.

This quilt has some interesting construction elements. The double window is unique. A stone arch is the primary window opening, which is embellished with an appliquéd floral arch. The grass layer is embroidered to give it a textured and realistic effect.

Finishing: 1-2-3

BACKING

Now that your top is complete, it is ready to be quilted. Prepare the top for sandwiching with a batting and a backing fabric. The choice of batting is a personal decision based on whether you hand or machine quilt or a combination of both. There are a great many different batts available, and your quilt shop can guide you in making a decision.

Choosing a backing gives you another opportunity to dip into your fabric collection. You can use the back of your quilt to make a spectacular statement, or you can use whatever fabric is at hand. Here are some possibilities:

Two-sided quilt – Double your pleasure by using another complete quilt top as the backing.

Complementary – Choose a backing fabric with a design that relates to the quilt top's theme.

Camouflage – A fabric with a busy print will mask quilting stitches while you learn new machine-quilting techniques.

Utilitarian – Use up yardage that's been taking up valuable space on your shelves. If you're wondering which fabrics are utilitarian, they're the ones you look at now and wonder why you ever bought them in the first place and why you bought so much of them.

QUILTING AND BINDING

You can choose to hand or machine quilt or both. This is an excellent opportunity to practice machine quilting and develop your skills. There are many books on the market to help you perfect your machine technique. This would be a good time to experiment with decorative stitches and the many threads available. With the new techniques presented in this book, you will produce so many new quilt tops in such a short time that machine quilting may be the most realistic way to quilt them as quickly as they are produced.

INSPIRATIONAL SCRAPBOOK

Each of these quilts will provide you with an assortment of inspirational ideas for your own Quilt With A View.

WHERE EAGLES SOAR

28" x 32", by Donna Howland, Intervale, New Hampshire.

This quilt is quite dramatic with its presentation of a majestic eagle soaring over a desert against a hand-painted stormy sky and the sun just breaking through. A partial floral wreath borders the foreground and balances the solid-fabric borders.

MY FATHER'S GARDEN

28" x 26", by Donna Howland, Intervale, New Hampshire.

Donna used a partial-circle opening against a sky background to frame a garden of irises reminiscent of her father's beautiful iris beds. Trapunto on some of the irises and the dimensional butterflies make the viewer want to reach out and pick a bloom.

THERE'S HOPE IN EACH NEW DAWN

12" x 10", by Lynn Collins, Kennebunk, Maine.

Lynn made this quilt as she was struggling with cancer. "I used the fabric medium as a tool to express hope both in the symbol of the sunrise and in my insistence on continuing to work on the piece," she says.

Author's note: As I looked at the quilt over and over again, I felt something was missing. I then did something I have never done before. I added something to someone else's work. With her approval, I quilted a golden sun with streaming rays of sunshine and hope breaking over the hills.

TROPICAL SUNSET

25" x 30", by Kathy Siuta, Cockeysville, Maryland.

Appliquéd tropical motifs against a hand-painted sunset sky allow the viewer to relax and enjoy this scene. The curve of the palm trees and the addition of the flying birds help the eye travel through the view. Kathy enjoyed the freedom this design allowed. She says, "I usually work with templates and exact placement lines. But it was so wonderful to just cut and sew whatever the fabric told me."

CAVE DIVE

35" x 33", by Mary Haunani Ceasar, Kailua, Hawaii.

This seascape quilt takes the viewer into the beautiful underwater world of the Pacific Ocean. French-ribbon seaweed, trapunto fish, beading, and inked details set against a brilliant hand-painted fabric give this quilt a realistic feeling. It's an underwater adventure without getting wet.

TROPICAL NIGHT

32" x 31", by Patt Wilson, Vancouver, British Columbia, Canada.

A large tropical print of foliage and parrots was Patt's inspiration for this quilt. A window opening was cut off-center and backed with a piece of fabric she had painted especially for this quilt. The jungle foliage breaks open against a dark starry sky, with just a few parrots taking it all in.

Greek Ruins

27" x 42", by Paula Butzi, Woodenville, Washington; hand-painted fabric by Mickey Lawler.

This picture fractures the window concept into ruins. Paula took apart a fabric printed with temple ruins and placed them on a hand-painted landscape fabric. Greek Ruins is a large piece that can be described as a linear landscape.

CACHETTE DE LA TIGRE/TIGER HIDING PLACE

46" x 54", by Gail Rowe, Southboro, Massachusetts.

CACHETTE DE LA TIGRE *was the result of using a large-scale floral print and a full-yard piece of a hand-painted sunset sky. Gail could not stop cutting openings in the foliage to view the sky.*

A WINDOW UNTO HEAVEN

41" x 45", by Ruth A.C. Haynes, Jefferson, Massachusetts.

The raw-edge appliqué allowed this piece to be constructed quickly. Ruth took two fabrics that were puzzling her and put them together. "Most of my friends would look at these fabrics and tell me to make an attic window or a tablecloth. Imagine my surprise when the fabrics mated perfectly."

RIVERS OF FLOWERS

19" x 19", by Persis Darling, Silver Spring, Maryland.

A print with an Oriental flavor was cut open along the design's meandering flowing lines. A hand-painted landscape fabric and inked birds take the viewer into the window and beyond the horizon.

TWO CRANES

30" x 31", by Judy Lundberg, Silver Spring, Maryland.

An Oriental fabric was cut following the path of flowers in the fabric's design. Two cranes, flying off into a hand-painted sunset, were beautifully inked. A simple picture-frame border, cut from a purple batik, is set off with a narrow white accent strip. This piece has an elegant simplicity.

PINK KIMONO

23" x 24", by Judy Lundberg, Silver Spring, Maryland.

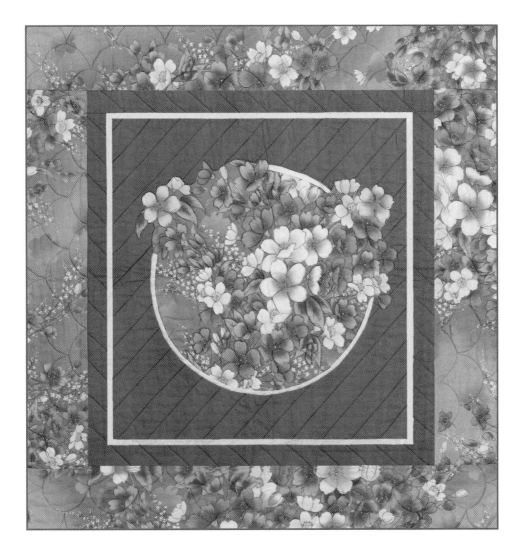

Judy reversed the roles of the window and view fabrics with this wonderful result. The floral view fabric spills out onto the simple round window opening. A white accent strip effectively highlights the window opening and the picture-frame border.

JAPANESE RIBBONS

25" x 23", by Judy Lundberg, Silver Spring, Maryland.

A solid black fabric with a circular opening focuses attention on a cascade of Japanese ribbons and blooms that have burst through and come forward to the border's edge. This is a dramatic presentation for a wonderfully rich Oriental print fabric.

IRISH II

32" x 32", by Georgette Sutton, Biddeford, Maine.

A round window opening spotlights a printed mountain view that was sparked to whimsical life with a holiday novelty fabric as the accent. The borders pick up the Irish theme with Flying Geese (looking for the pot of gold?) and a field of shamrocks surrounding them. There are many wonderful holiday fabrics to inspire seasonal Quilts With A View.

CHRISTMAS IN TOYLAND

30" x 31", by the author; quilted by Ellen Peters.

A window fabric of Christmas-tree decorations was free-cut to reveal a view of a Christ-mas village. The block is bordered on two sides with more tree decorations, while the remaining sides are bordered with fabric that pulls the view scene into the borders. Using wide borders causes a block to grow large quickly and easily.

LITTLE CABIN IN THE WOODS

26" x 24", by the author.

A winter landscape was easily created by cutting a printed fabric along the snow line and silhouetting it against a starry night sky through snowy woods. These two fabrics blend beautifully. The starry sky was embellished with sparkling beads for a glittery, snowflake effect. The quilt was bordered with theme fabrics: holly leaves, berries, and snowflakes against a night sky.

HYAKUTAKE

23" x 28", by Berta Murray, Hyattsville, Maryland.

An arched window opening takes the viewer into an exotic Mid-Eastern view. A whole-cloth scene was cut along the roof tops and appliquéd against a dark starry sky. The quilt was embellished with beads and dimensional olive leaves. This quilt was named for HYAKUTAKE, a comet that appeared in the sky at the time Berta was making this quilt.

Resources

FABRICS

Skydyes
PO Box 370116
West Hartford, CT 06117
Hand-painted cottons and silks

Shades Hand Dyed Textiles
585 Cobb Parkway S., Nunn Complex
Marietta, GA 30062
Hand-dyed fabrics

Hancock's of Paducah
3841 Hinkleville Rd.
Paducah, KY 42001
Mail-order catalog

Keepsake Quilting
PO Box 1618
Centre Harbor, NH 03226-1618
Mail-order catalog

Quilts & Other Comforts
B2500
Louisiana, MO 63353-7500
Mail-order catalog

Quilt Artisan
747 Aquidneck Ave.
Middletown, RI 02840
Fabrics and supplies for quilters

TEACHERS

Ellen Peters
27 Tremont St.
Laconia, NH 03246
603-524-6956
Fax: 603-524-7282
Workshops, professional quilting

Faye Labanaris
80 Mt. Vernon St.
Dover, NH 03820
603-742-0211
Fax: 603-740-9199
Workshops, lectures, trunk shows, and
French ribbon and flower-making supplies

Mickey Lawler
PO Box 370116
W. Hartford, CT 06117
Workshops, lectures

About the Author

A professional quilt teacher since 1990, Faye has taught at major quilt conferences. Her specialties are Baltimore album appliqué, Hawaiian quilting, and dimensional French ribbon flowers. Her quilt, A TRIBUTE TO CELIA THAXTER, won first place in the category Reflective of a Particular Life and Time in C&T's Baltimore Album Revival Contest in 1994. Faye was also voted National Honored Teacher of Baltimore Album Appliqué by her students in that same contest.

After being introduced to French ribbon work in Elly Sienkiewicz's *Dimensional Appliqué*, Faye began intensely working with this new material. She lavishly incorporated wire-edged ribbon flowers into her CELIA THAXTER quilt for a realistic and unique appearance. Her first book, *Blossoms by the Sea* (AQS, 1996), tells the story of Celia Thaxter's life, garden, the quilt, and making the flowers from the quilt.

"I enjoy the freedom of creativity and spontaneity that the French ribbon flower technique provides," Faye says. "I have developed many original flowers and quilt designs for my workshops. I enjoy teaching people to have fun with their work and strive for class participants to achieve successful results and personal satisfaction."

Faye's second quilting love is Hawaiian quiltmaking. She was introduced to it at the first Great American Quilt Festival in New York City in 1986. After studying under master Hawaiian quiltmakers Elizabeth Akana and Mealii Kalama in Hawaii, she began teaching this beautiful form of quiltmaking throughout New England. It was her love of Hawaiian quilts and Hawaii that led to the development of QUILT HAWAII, a quilt conference held on a different island each year since 1992.

Faye began quilting in 1976 and was twice a state winner in the Great American Quilt Festival's contests, Memories of Childhood and Discover America. Faye lives in Dover, New Hampshire. She is married and has two grown sons. She has a college degree and taught biology and marine biology at Dover High School for eight years before leaving to raise her family. Since that time, she has also been a science consultant for the Dover Elementary Schools. She now travels and teaches quilters throughout the United States, Canada, and Europe.

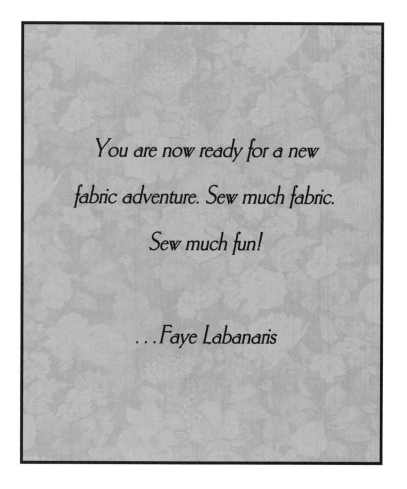

You are now ready for a new

fabric adventure. Sew much fabric.

Sew much fun!

. . .Faye Labanaris

AQS Books on Quilts

This is only a partial listing of the books on quilts that are available from the American Quilter's Society. AQS books are known the world over for their timely topics, clear writing, beautiful color photographs, and accurate illustrations and patterns. The following books are available from your local bookseller, quilt shop, or public library. If you are unable to locate certain titles in your area, you may order by mail from the AMERICAN QUILTER'S SOCIETY, P.O. Box 3290, Paducah, KY 42002-3290. Add $2.00 for postage for the first book ordered and 40¢ for each additional book. Include item number, title, and price when ordering. Allow 14 to 21 days for delivery. Customers with Visa, MasterCard, or Discover may phone in orders from 7:00–5:00 CST, Monday–Friday, Toll Free 1-800-626-5420.